Greater Than a Tourist - Guadalajara Mexico

50 Travel Tips from a Local

Juan Uribe

Order Information: To order this title please email lbrenenc@gmail.com or visit GreaterThanATourist.com. A bulk discount can be provided.

Cover Template Creator: Lisa Rusczyk Ed. D. using Canva.
Cover Creator:
Image:

Lock Haven, PA
All rights reserved.
ISBN: 9781549881848

>TOURIST

BOOK DESCRIPTION

Are you excited about planning your next trip?

Do you want to try something new?

Would you like some guidance from a local?

If you answered yes to any of these questions, then this
Greater Than a Tourist book is for you.

Greater Than a Tourist – Guadalajara, by Juan Uribe offers the
inside scoop on Guadalajara. Most travel books tell you how to
sightsee. Although there's nothing wrong with that, as a part of the
Greater than a Tourist series, this book will give you tips from
someone who lives at your next travel destination. In these pages,
you'll discover local advice that will help you throughout your trip.
Travel like a local. Slow down and get to know the people and the
culture of a place. By the time you finish this book, you will be
eager and prepared to travel to your next destination.

TABLE OF CONTENTS

DEDICATION

This book is dedicated to family and friends who have always supported me and stayed by my side no matter what.

Infinite gratitude.

It is also dedicate to all those Mexicans who lost their lives in the earthquake that hit Mexico on September 19th 2017, you will forever be in our memories.

ABOUT THE AUTHOR

Juan Uribe is a writer who lives in Guadalajara and has an enormous passion for the city.

But that doesn't mean he never leaves town, he loves to travel and one of his goals is to visit every state in Mexico.

He's been living in Guadalajara since 1994 and he is happy to call it home.

HOW TO USE THIS BOOK

The Greater Than a Tourist book series was written by someone who has lived in an area for over three months. The goal of this book is to help travelers either dream or experience different locations by providing opinions from a local. The author has made suggestions based on their own experiences. Please do your own research before traveling to the area in case the suggested places are unavailable.

FROM THE PUBLISHER

Traveling can be one of the most important parts of a person's life. The anticipation and memories that you have are some of the best. As a publisher of the Greater Than a Tourist book series, as well as the popular 50 Things to Know book series, we strive to help you learn about new places, spark your imagination, and inspire you. Wherever you are and whatever you do I wish you safe, fun, and inspiring travel.

Lisa Rusczyk Ed. D.

CZYK Publishing

WELCOME TO > TOURIST

INTRODUCTION

Guadalajara is one of Mexico's most beautiful cities, it combines the country's most famous symbols (mariachi and tequila) with tradition and the fast paced and modern lifestyle that big urban cities have embraced.

I've been an amateur tour guide for family and friends that have come to visit our beloved "Pear of the West" and they have all left town with a positive opinion of this marvelous city.

This book is a reflection of my personal experience only.

1. Souvenirs To Bring Back Home

Buying souvenirs in Guadalajara is very easy because you get to choose from a great variety of typical products of the region. The obvious choices are food and drinks, and Guadalajara has some very special treats. Tequila is the way to go if you want to buy alcoholic beverages, this liquor is famous around the world and it is from the state of Jalisco, so it's a great gift of overall quality.

Art is another popular gift and souvenir that visitors love to take back home for friends or themselves. It really depends on what you are looking for, but you can find interesting things in Tonalá or Tlaquepaque, their local markets have an incredible variety of art that is very appreciated around the planet.

Other options are music and books, Guadalajara has a long tradition of great musicians and writers, you can by a record or a book at very good price, lower than what could find online, so this is a great option as well.

2. Pictures To Take In Guadalajara

One of the most amazing and breathtaking aspects of Guadalajara is that it combines the beauty of a traditional Mexican city and the exciting lifestyle of a modern metropolis, this means that we have an amazing variety of places we can take pictures of. A good start is downtown, where you can find many historic buildings that are hundreds of years old.

We have modern buildings in very prosperous areas, like in Andares and Puerta de Hierro, where all the thriving businesses have opened their offices. Other interesting sites to take pictures are the Matute Remus bridge at night, and the town centers of Zapopan and Tlaquepaque, cities that are part of the metropolitan area.

If you are into sports you'll have a great time taking pictures at our three major sports venues: Estadio Jalisco, Estadio Omnilife, and Estadio Charros.

3. How To Get Around In Guadalajara

There are multiple ways to get around in Guadalajara and usually, it's inexpensive. The preferred transport of most "tapatíos" is the bus because it is are cheap and you don't have to wait for much to board one.

Another way to get around town in the city's metro system that will have a new third line open and running in 2018. As of now the metro has two lines, one crosses the city from north to south, and the second line goes from downtown to the eastern part of the city.

If you want a faster and private way to move around you can take a yellow cab or if you have the app there is Uber available. The cost is almost the same nowadays, so either one will do if you are in a hurry.

Getting around Guadalajara is very easy and there are plenty of options depending on your budget, some of the sights to see are even in a walking distance.

4. Why Visit Guadalajara?

I am really convinced that Guadalajara is a wonderful city, as I have already mentioned before, we have the best of two worlds, the city has a rich five hundred year history and that is part of our lifestyle, but modern trends have their own place as well and we enjoy being part of a global town that is home for people from all over the world.

As a Mexican who has traveled around his own country I know that Mexico is very diverse, there are many cultures and ideologies that are alive and well in our territory, but it is exact to say that the country's most representative symbols are from Jalisco and its capital, Guadalajara.

If there is such thing as a "Mexican city" it would certainly be Guadalajara, you can drink a tequila listening to live mariachi and know that you are in the right place. You can't go wrong visiting our city, you'll like it and understand why it's such a popular destination.

5. Best Times To Visit Guadalajara

I'm tempted to say that any time of year is great to visit Guadalajara, the city had a well-earned reputation as a place with the kindest weather, but that has changed over the last few years, so it really depends on what your interests are.

If you don't mind the rain then you can visit at any time, but if want to avoid precipitation then do not come to Guadalajara in the summertime, it does not rain every day but we do have some very aggressive thunderstorms very often during that time of the year.

April, May, and June are very hot and dry months, so if you don't like elevated temperatures you could pick another month to come. The winter is almost non-existing, it never really is cold in Guadalajara, if you are from a place that is normally cold then you'll feel it is summer.

My favorite months in this city are September, October, and March, but feel free to visit anytime.

6. Currency to carry

I know that in many other parts of the world you can get along just fine with a piece a plastic, be it a credit or debit card, with cash being almost obsolete, but that is not the case in Guadalajara, and certainly not in most places in Mexico.

There are many establishments, stores, restaurants, and services that will gladly accept payment with plastic, but there are many other businesses that only accept cash, so you'll need to carry some at all times. It doesn't mean that you have to take a bag of money everywhere you go, but enough to buy yourself a nice meal and a safe ride home (if you have Uber installed on your phone then you have that covered).

And when I say that you have to carry money I'm talking about Mexican pesos; dollars, euros, or any other currency will not be accepted to prevent money laundering, so you'll need to exchange your currency before you can go on an adventure in my beloved city.

7. Where To Stay In Guadalajara

There are many nice hotels to stay in Guadalajara, and there are options for all types of budgets. You can stay downtown, there many low cost options, but you can also find the famous chain hotels that you see in cities all over the world.

Some hotels in downtown Guadalajara are not cheap and they are not the typical Best Western or Holiday Inn, there are precious and historic buildings that have been adapted and modified to serve as comfortable hotels.

But the ideal hotel really depends on what you are in Guadalajara for, the reason of your visit. If you are in town for a specific event then the best option is to stay in a hotel close to the venue, because Guadalajara is a huge city and it wouldn't make sense to cross town in rush hour.

The hotel infrastructure in Guadalajara is enough to host big events and accommodate tourists from all types of financial capacities, being a large metropolis has some advantages.

8. What To Eat

In Mexico we love to eat, it is part of our culture and lifestyle. For Mexicans eating spicy food is something we do almost every single day, we eat it since we are babies.

I can only imagine the problem it represents from people from other countries, running away and avoiding spicy food. As an amateur tour guide I know for sure that everyone falls in the involuntary trap and ends up getting "enchilado", it is so fun.

I wrote this because if you come to Guadalajara you have to eat our traditional meals (going to McDonald's is not an option), and some of them are spicy even without the extra chili. That being said, you need to eat: tortas ahogadas, birria, tacos de barbacoa, pozole, and many other traditional meals, but don't worry, I'll get into more details later. You just need to be open to new flavors and sensations, I assure you that it would be worthwhile.

9. What To Drink

Drinks are one the most important aspects of a travel adventure, and not necessarily alcoholic drinks. First of all, you always need to drink bottled water, never tap water. You won't die if you drink tap water, but I don't want any stomach infections hampering your visit to Guadalajara.

Once I got this out of the way, I'll go with other types of beverages. If you're into the partying aspect of the trip then I'm are happy to tell you that there are many different types of liquor that you can try.

Probably you already know that tequila is what "Mexican machos" enjoy, well yes, they do. But you can also try mezcal, raicilla, and pulque. The first two can be found in bars, while pulque is not that popular. It can be found in traditional markets as a day beverage, something to help you get by the day.

And yes, there is a great beer selection as well.

10. Try Mezcal And Raicilla

In this tip, I'll go further to explain what mezcal, raicilla, and pulque are. These alcoholic beverages are as Mexican as any other, so they deserve to be written about.

I can say that mezcal is a cousin of tequila, because they are both made from agave. But the difference is that a different type of agave for each one, for tequila blue agave is the choice, while agave espadín is used for mezcal.

The same can be said for raicilla, it is also made from a type of agave called maximiliana. Both mezcal and raicilla have become very popular in recent years, people who only a few years ago would have felt insulted if they were offered these types of drinks now consider them something fashionable to drink.

Most mezcal is elaborated in Oaxaca but is popular nationwide, while raicilla is from Jalisco and still is relatively unknown outside of the state.

"Nothing can last forever. There isn't any memory,

no matter how intense, that doesn't fade out at last".

—Juan Rulfo

11. Places To Walk in Guadalajara

One of the reasons I love Guadalajara is that it is so easy to walk in downtown and in the Americana neighborhood.

The best time of day to walk around downtown is in the morning or the evening, there are many sites to see and it would be nearly impossible to drive in that area, so like it or not walking will always be the best option.

In the Americana neighborhood, the best time to walk is in the night, because of all the nightlife and social interaction in the streets. You find dancing lessons, book sales, and many other cultural manifestations, there is always something new.

But there are many other places where you can enjoy a good walk. In the Providencia neighborhood you can take a long walk, especially in Pablo Neruda Avenue, it's a great place to make some exercise as well.

You can also enjoy a pleasant walk in Zapopan and Tlaquepaque.

12. Places To See In Guadalajara

This tip will be more like an introduction or general overview for some of the ones to come. Like in all tourist adventures, the places to see really depend on the interest and preferences of the traveler.

The budget and lifestyle are linked and determine the places you'll end up visiting. You can find almost anything in Guadalajara, so if you are someone that is looking for fine dinners and expensive clubs you'll get them.

If your trip is more on the cultural side, you'll find historic buildings that are invaluable to human heritage. In the local markets you'll be able to eat traditional dishes at very low prices.

If you can't live without shopping malls, we have those too, we have Andares, Galerías, La Gran Plaza, Forum, Ciudadela, and much more.

Guadalajara has something for everyone.

13. Places To Shop In Guadalajara

Guadalajara is a great city for shopping. I already mentioned the shopping malls, and Andares is probably the fanciest one. It is located in the richest zone of the city and is one of the most visited places in town because it also has a great variety of restaurants.

But in shopping malls, you'll find products that you can find anywhere in the world, and that's not what traveling is about. If you want to go local then you need to go to the markets that are distributed all over the city, almost every community has one.

The most famous markets are the ones that are in or close to downtown, like San Juan de Dios, Santa Tere, Alcalde, Juárez, Mexicaltinzgo, or Corona. These are probably the best places to buy souvenirs or to have a bite. The food in the markets is usually very good and inexpensive, and it doesn't get better than that.

14. Nightlife In Guadalajara

Nightlife in Guadalajara is amazing, seriously, there is always something to do, a new bar to visit, a party to attend, concerts, you name it and we have it.

The star of the city's nightlife is Chapultepec Avenue, there is no doubt about it. The most trendy bars are located in this area and there is a great variety of options for all shapes and sizes, you can find bars that play live music, rock, banda, salsa, cumbia, electronic, etc.

In downtown Guadalajara you can find the traditional cantinas, some of them are more than one hundred years old, but I'll talk more about them later, they deserve a more detailed explanation.

There are also high-profile nightclubs like La Santa, Bosse, and other popular spots where the bouncer is the man of the hour and decides who parties and who doesn't.

15. Festivals In Guadalajara

Guadalajara is one of Mexico's most important cities, and it hosts several important festivals. The most important ones are the Guadalajara Book Festival and the Guadalajara International Film Festival, but those deserve their own tip, so you'll get to know more about them later.

Music festivals are also very popular in Guadalajara and some are becoming attractive for music lovers from all over the country. Rock festivals have been a success in the city, Roxy, Festival de Mayo, Revolution Fest, and Coordenada have drawn immense crowds confirming the city's appetite for big events.

Mariachi also has its own celebration in August and September, mariachis from all over the planet gather in a festival that lasts for days and has its own parade.

Last but not least we have the city fair that is scheduled for October every year, called "Fiestas de Octubre".

16. Learn Some Phrases In Spanish

It always helps to know some Spanish to help you get around, you can learn some basic phrases, I will start with greetings: Hola (hello), buenos días (good morning), buenas tardes (good afternoon), buenas noches (good night), ¿cómo está? (how are you), por favor (please).

Directions are always useful as well starting with the basic: ¿Dónde está? (where is?), ¿dónde está el baño? (where is the bathroom?), a la izquierda (to the left), a la derecha (to the right), derecho (straight ahead), en la esquina (in the corner), en el norte (in the north), en el sur (in the south).

And I know that you'll eventually get hungry, so here go the must know phrases for restaurants: Una mesa (a table), un menú (a menu), hamburguesa (hamburger), sopa (soup), ensalada (salad), agua (water), cerveza (beer), café (coffee), la cuenta (the check).

With this vocabulary you will be just fine.

17. Buy Some Groceries

Guadalajara is a big town and there all types of options for grocery shopping. The obvious options are the supermarkets, where you can find almost everything, the biggest are: Walmart, Sam's, Costco, Comercial Mexicana, Chedraui, Aurrerá, and Soriana.

You can also buy your groceries in the local markets, where they have fresh fruit, vegetables, and butcheries. There is one big market that is called "Mercado de Abastos", you can get great prices and you can buy wholesale if that is necessary.

But in Guadalajara you don't need to go that far to buy one or two grocery products, there are local convenience stores that are called "tiendas de la esquina" (corner shops) that have almost anything you need, the catch is that it's always more expensive than in the supermarket, but it's very useful when you are in a hurry or the supermarket is too far away.

Oxxo and Seven-Eleven are always nearby as well.

18. Remember To Bring These Items With You

Depending on the time of year you will need to bring some specific articles, but nothing special, they are stuff that maybe you already had thought of.

If you come to Guadalajara in the summer you must bring raincoats, rain boots, and umbrellas. The thunderstorms in this city are something spectacular, but sometimes not in a good way, so you need to be prepared for excessive amounts of rain. But that does not mean that you don't need some sunscreen, because the city is very hot in the summer, beginning in May.

In Guadalajara you will walk a lot, so I recommend you bring comfortable clothing and shoes. Winters are not very harsh, but in December and January you'll be better off wearing a sweater.

And don't forget to bring cash with you, because you will need it at some point.

19. Stay Safe In Guadalajara

Like any major city in the world, Guadalajara has its own crime issues and you should take the necessary precautions. I recommend that past 10:00 PM you stay away from places like Plaza Tapatía and San Juan de Dios. These places are tourist sites by day but very dangerous at night.

There are never guarantees, but it is still safer to travel through vehicles hailed from apps like Uber, Easy Taxi, Cabify, and City Drive. If you go out late at night these are your best options to go back to the hotel safely.

Other useful advice that I can give you is not to carry too much cash with you, I know that I have made emphasis in that you need cash to move around, but that doesn't mean that you have to carry hundreds of dollars. Take enough to get you through the day.

Also, I strongly advise not to wear expensive jewelry, because it will bring too much unnecessary attention to yourself.

20. Move Around In Guadalajara's Train Lines

I already mentioned the city's electric train lines before, but in this tip I'll go more into details. This transportation system has two lines as of 2017, with a third one being built for 2018. Line 1 has twelve stations, while Line 2 has ten stations. The first line goes from north to south and back, while the second one goes from downtown to the east and back.

Juárez Station in Line 1 and Plaza Universidad in Line 2 are the ones that leave you in downtown Guadalajara. Another popular station in Line 2 is San Juan de Dios, thousands of people go to Latin America's biggest market, and you should give it a try as well.

Guadalajara's electric train is the city's best transportation system by far, it is clean and fast, it is also very comfortable and very dependable. If you have the chance try it out, even if is just for fun, maybe you can make it an adventure of its own.

"Did you know we know we are all the

object of another's imagination?"

— *Carlos Fuentes*

21. Enjoy The Romería In October

The Romería is a major event here in Guadalajara, maybe the biggest of them all. Some statistics say that more one million people gather to see the Virgin of Zapopan travel from Guadalajara's Cathedral to Zapopan on October 12th. The distance from one temple to another is eight kilometers or approximately five miles.

This is a very old tradition that has its origins in the Jewish culture and was brought to the American continent by the Spaniard priests. In Guadalajara, this tradition started in 1695 and has not lost any of its popularity ever since.

The Virgin of Zapopan is escorted to its home by dancers called the "danzantes", who dress in indigenous clothing and dance all night and day, they train all year to be ready for this event.

If you happen to be in the city in October do not forget to be part of this enormous event.

22. Guadalajara Is Full Of Libraries

The city's libraries are an important part of its history, we have one main library that is Jalisco's Public Library, it has a new building to call home on the northern side of town, it used to be in front of Agua Azul Park just south of downtown.

University of Guadalajara has huge libraries in each of its campuses, these are specialized and are a very useful for researchers, students, and the general public that want to find very specific information.

The most beautiful library of Guadalajara is in Plaza Universidad, the Spanish American (Iberoamericana in Spanish) Library is located inside of an old traditional building and it is a great place to read quietly and admire the architecture of the site. The library has a neoclassical façade that is so characteristic of the buildings in downtown Guadalajara.

Even if you aren't into reading it will be totally worth your time, so go check it out if you have a chance.

23. Don't Miss Out On The Traditional "Cantinas"

Guadalajara is full of Mexican traditions and one of the best is the existence of cantinas, a type of bar where you can eat and drink a beer or any other alcoholic drink.

As you can already imagine, most of them are located downtown and are very old. For example, La Fuente opened its doors and started serving drinks in 1921, it is famous for a bicycle that a client left there and never came back for. You can see the bike hanging on the wall waiting for its owner to come back for it.

Other famous and popular cantinas are Bar Martín, Bar Zapotlán, Los Famosos Equipales, Morelias, Iberia, Gran Chavarín, La Cava, Mascusia República, and Bar Gil. Each one of them has their own personality and history, long history.

They serve traditional beverages and appetizers that you won't find in any other bars, cantinas are definitely places that you have to visit if you are in Guadalajara.

24. Cabañas Is One The Best Sites In Town

The Hospicio Cabañas is a neoclassic style building that is one of Guadalajara's most emblematic symbols. Just as you might have guessed by the name, this place was a hospice from 1810 to 1980.

The hospice is famous because of the murals José Clemente Orozco painted in the inside walls, and it was declared as World Heritage in 1997 by the UNESCO. The murals were painted from 1938 to 1939 and the most impressive one is the "Man on Fire".

This historic building even played a role in two of the biggest events in Mexican history. In 1810, in the war for the Mexican Independence it became a military base for the royal troops; and 1910, in the Mexican Revolution it also became headquarters for the federal troops.

With no more children to foster, the place is now a cultural center, with movie projections and art galleries.

25. Speaking Of Murals…

The muralist movement that reached its height in the early-mid portion of the past century is one of Mexico's most important contributions to contemporary culture, and Guadalajara has murals of some of the most famous painters of the movement.

I already mentioned Orozco's famous murals in Hospicio Cabañas, but there are other important paintings distributed in the city's buildings.

David Alfaro Siqueiros painted a mural inside the Spanish American Library in 1926-1927 that represents the Marxist ideals, with depictions of the workers, farmers, miners, and artisans in their efforts to collect the fruit from nature.

Prominent muralist Gabriel Flores has various paintings in the city's traditional buildings, his work can be found in Salvador Allende Auditorium, the old Public Library, the Experimental Theater of Jalisco, and the administrative building of the University of Guadalajara.

26. Guadalajara And Its Museums

As you would expect from a city like Guadalajara, there are very important museums that you can and should visit in your time in town.

I already mentioned Hospicio Cabañas and in a way it can be considered the most important of them all because of the murals, but other museums are very important to the city's cultural landscape.

"Museo de las Artes" is an important museum because it is funded by the University of Guadalajara and always has world-class art exhibitions. Another great museum is the city's paleontology museum, they have some impressive exhibits of the animals that roamed these lands thousands of years ago.

In the northern part of the city there is a museum made for kids called "Trompo Mágico", it is very modern and science-oriented, it is one Guadalajara's most famous cultural venues.

27. Take A Ride In The New Calandrias

Calandrias are little carts that up until 2017 were pulled by horses. They had been part of the city's traditions for decades, but the municipal government decided to retire the horses and put motorized wagons instead.

The decision was very popular but it also faced some criticism. Calandrias were a fixture in the downtown and rides were very popular, tourists and locals loved them equally.

This tradition has its origins in the twentieth century and it is a job that is passed from generation to generation. The ride consists of a small tour of the most important sites in the downtown area with the explanation from the driver.

The sites you get to see are Teatro Degollado, Plaza Liberación, Plaza de Armas, Parque Agua Azul, Ex Convento del Carmen, Plaza Revolución, and the offices of University of Guadalajara.

The motorized tour will lose the traditional appeal, but the horses will finally catch a break.

28. Time To Eat: The Famous Torta Ahogada

The torta ahogada is Guadalajara's most traditional dish, and it cannot get more "tapatío" than this, as it was created in the downtown area.

The torta ahogada is a piece a bread that is filled with fried pork meat and bathed in tomato sauce, that is where the name comes from (ahogada means drowned), some places serve the torta with fried beans.

Everybody has their own favorite spot to eat torta ahogada, some of the most popular places are Tortas Toño, Don José, Las Famosas, Mr. Paco's, and El Príncipe Heredero; but you can find them almost in any area in town.

What makes this dish so special is that you can only eat it in Guadalajara because the climate is ideal for the type of bread that is used for the torta, called "birote salado". There is no other place in the country that can replicate the flavor, so if you want a real torta ahogada you must eat it in Guadalajara and no place else.

29. Guadalajara Is A Great Place To Eat Birria

Birria is another traditional Mexican dish and Guadalajara is a great place to eat it. The basic recipe is meat and a mixture of tomato, chili, and spices. You can eat it dry or in broth, there are different ways to prepare it. You'll find birria in small and big restaurants all over the city, and it is delicious.

There are many famous spots where you can try very good birria, the most prestigious place might be El Chololo, a restaurant located in Tlaquepaque, but I must say that it is far from the downtown area, so you'll need to hail a ride or have some acquaintance give you a lift.

Other great places to have a plate of birria are the restaurants that are located in the Nine Corners, a popular plaza just south of downtown, you can't go wrong with any of them, be it El Compadre, El Paisano, or any other.

Another area in town with good birria is the Santa Tere neighborhood, with La Victoria and El Torito serving awesome meals.

30. Admire The City's Beautiful Buildings

This tip is closely related to a couple others I've mentioned before, but with new and different buildings and monuments that are worth visiting.

Guadalajara's cathedral is one of the city's most iconic buildings, it is the center of the religious life on this side of the country, it has a great history and is a must-see for all tourists.

The Matute Remus bridge is relatively new and in a short span of time has become one of Guadalajara's most beautiful sites, especially at night, when the bridge is illuminated with colorful lights.

And now we go to another church, a gothic styled building that is one of the favorites of the people of Guadalajara, the Templo Expiatorio is one of the most beautiful religious sites in town, you'll love it. It's in downtown, so it's easy to access.

"What distinguishes modern art from the

art of other ages is criticism".

— Octavio Paz

31. Visit More Buildings And Monuments!

The last tip was not nearly enough to mention the great buildings that you have to visit while in Guadalajara.

Towards the western part of the downtown area there are two of the city's most emblematic monuments: Los Arcos and La Minerva. Both are located close to each other in Vallarta Avenue.

Los Arcos (the arches) was built in 1942, they are two neoclassic arches that were intended to be a welcome sign for visitors, then a few decades later the city grew so much that the arches are in an area that is considered centric.

The Minerva is only a few meters away from Los Arcos and is the biggest fountain in the city. In the middle of the fountain, there is a 74 meters high statue of the roman goddess Minerva. This may very well be the city's most beloved monument, a divine figure that is the custodian of the city.

Don't forget to take lots of pictures in all these sites!

32. Go To Panteón De Belén

Panteón de Belen (cemetery of Belén) is a historic and cultural landmark in Guadalajara, it was built in 1848 and was closed in 1896, it's really small and reached its maximum capacity in short period of time. Many important people from that era were buried in this cemetery: politicians, musicians, scientists, writers, and wealthy people.

Some of the tombs are spectacular, real works of art that are part of the city's heritage. Nowadays it's a cultural center where you'll be able to see plays and art exhibitions. One of the most popular activities in Panteón de Belén are the tours organized at night, in these tours the guide explains the origin of some of the most luxurious tombs and also some of the legends that have made the cemetery one of the most famous sites in the city.

It's worth noting that Panteón de Belén is not a horror house, it is a very important cultural site that is preserved as such. It really is worth your while, so go check it out!

33. Visit Guadalajara's Traditional Coffee Shops

I think I've made it clear by now, Guadalajara is a city full of marvelous traditions, but time brings change and what used to be a quiet and laid back city is now a frenetic metropolis. The traditional coffee shops from downtown Guadalajara are a testament to that lifestyle, but they have lost a lot of customers thanks to new types of coffee businesses.

But some of these coffee joints are still alive and are a window that lets you go back in time and see how "tapatíos" used to live a couple of decades ago, you'll see old men playing dominos and chess, couples having a drink or even dinner. These are places where time goes by slower, they are not hostages of tight schedules.

The most famous coffee shops are: Flor de Córdoba, Café Madrid, Café Madoka, Café La Parroquia, and Café Zapopan.

34. Enjoy The "Vía Recreativa" On Sundays

The "Vía Recreativa" is a social program in which important streets and avenues from all over the city are made available for walking, bike rides, roller skating, skateboarding and all other vehicles that do not use a motor, this is done on Sundays and people from all over town take to the streets.

In downtown Guadalajara, you can rent bikes and enjoy a ride or you can just walk, it is about taking back the city for a few hours. This program started back in September of 2004 with the idea of leaving the car at home at least one day a week.

The original route starts in Tetlán, the last train station on Line 2 of the electric train and ends at Los Arcos. In 2007 Zapopan joined the project and the routes have increased and really give the city a rest from pollution.

35. Do Some Shopping In Mercado Libertad (Or San Juan De Dios)

I've already mentioned this market in other tips, but it really is so important that it needs to be addressed separately. This market is located in the eastern part of the downtown area and it is the biggest indoors market of Latin America, it was inaugurated in 1958 and has been important in the life of city ever since.

You can go shopping or just see what it's all about, you'll find clothing, shoes, movies, video games, electronic devices, traditional candy, butcheries, fruits and vegetables, and little restaurants that serve Mexican food. The market has three levels and in each one of them different types articles can be found, food is served on the second floor for example; clothing, shoes, software and electronics on the third floor; while jewelry, candy, and crafts are sold in the first floor. You can find very nice souvenirs to take home in this market.

36. Plaza Tapatía, The Connection Between The Cathedral And Hospicio Cabañas

This public space was built in 1982 with a clear idea in mind, and that was to unite the prosper part of town, the west; with the east, where the poor people of Guadalajara live, like I said, that was the idea.

As anyone would expect, that just did not happen, but Plaza Tapatía has its importance in Guadalajara, it serves as a public space and it connects Guadalajara´s cathedral, Hospicio Cabañas, and Mercado Libertad. Not bad at all.

By day it is a lively place with all types of stores and it has a beautiful fountain that is, in fact, a mirror where you can see the reflection of the Hospicio Cabañas. Plaza Tapatía contains other smaller plazas, like Fundadores, Degollado, Explanada Central, and Paseo del Hospicio. This is definitely a site to see in Guadalajara.

37. The Beautiful Tlaquepaque

A place as beautiful as Tlaquepaque should have a better title to the tip, but it is just how I feel about this place, it is my favorite place in the city, the food is great, the ice cream, the Parían has a great Mexican vibe, the art galleries are incredible, it is a very special place.

The Parían is one of the most recognizable sites in downtown Tlaquepaque, it is a building with bars and restaurants that are connected to each other and serve Mexican food while a live mariachi plays in the background. This place is a favorite of locals and tourists alike.

Outside of El Parían is the garden, Jardín Hidalgo, a gorgeous typical Mexican plaza that is the gathering point and where you can find the food stands.

There is a pedestrian street that connects everything and has bars, art galleries, and gift shops. It is always a very colorful walk, don't you dare leave the city without visiting Tlaquepaque.

38. Tonalá Has Crafts For Everyone

Tonalá is municipality in the eastern part of the city's metropolitan area, it might not be the prettiest, but it does have something that everybody values, and that is crafts of all types, you can find expensive and artistic crafts, and you can find cheap and inexpensive crafts that can be useful around the house and kitchen. You decide what to buy.

The best days to go to Tonalá are Thursday and Sunday, those are the days the tianguis is installed and you can find a greater variety of crafts and souvenirs. It gets really crowded, so you have to be patient and with time to spare, because you'll need at least a couple of hours to walk through the entire tianguis.

Tonalá has a very important place in the city's history because it is one of the places where the founders tried to establish Guadalajara, but they encountered severe resistance from the local indigenous tribes, so they left for a less violent place to found the future Guadalajara.

39. Zapopan Has It All, Come Visit!

The fact that I live in Zapopan doesn't mean I'll exaggerate how great this municipality is, or maybe just a little. But the truth is that Zapopan does have some very important sites and it does have everything you can ask from a modern but traditional metropolis.

Downtown Zapopan has a pedestrian street that leads to the Basilica, and that street has an enormous arch built by the Spaniards that paves the way. The Zapopan Art Museum is located in that same street and I highly recommend you visit the exhibits. The road ends in the Basilica of Zapopan, a spectacular church that is visited by thousands of people every day and that hosts the end of the Romería in October.

Plaza de las Américas is just in front of the Basilica and it is nice place to sit down and relax, you can buy a delicious tejuino and drink it watching people pass by, or you can buy some pulque in the market that is on the other side of Hidalgo Avenue, it really depends on your mood.

40. Watch A Football (Soccer) Game In One Of The Most Modern Stadiums Of Latin America

Estadio Chivas is one of the premier venues in all of Mexico and Latin America. You guessed right, it is located in Zapopan and it is home to one of the most popular clubs of the country: Club Deportivo Guadalajara, also known as Chivas. The design is based on a volcano with a cloud on top of it, it's really unique.

The outer part of the stadium is covered with grass, that helps regulate the temperature inside the building. The capacity is 45 thousand seated fans, but for concerts, it can accommodate more people.

The stadium was inaugurated in July of 2010 in a friendly match between Chivas and Manchester United. The now world famous striker Javier "Chicharito" Hernández played in that game, and more recently (May 2017) Chivas won the league championship in this venue.

"Beyond myself, somewhere,

I wait for my arrival."

— Octavio Paz

41. Watch A Football (Soccer) Game In One Of The Most Traditional Stadiums Of Mexico

Before Chivas built its own stadium, Estadio Jalisco was home to three of the four traditional clubs in the city. Since the red and white club moved out its Atlas and Leones Negros the teams that play in this historic venue.

Estadio Jalisco is the third biggest stadium in Mexico and was opened in 1959. It has hosted games for two World Cups, in 1970 and 1986. The vibe on game days is something special, a type of social gathering with all the food vendors installed on the streets and people arriving from all the surrounding neighborhoods.

This stadium is very easy to access because it's located on Calzada Independencia, one of the most important avenues in the city. If you are in town during football (soccer) season I highly recommend you pay Estadio Jalisco a visit, it will be a great experience.

42. Go Watch a Charros Baseball Game!

Guadalajara has always been a football town, but it also has an important baseball tradition. Charros is the city's team and it came back for the 2014 Mexican Pacific League season after the Summer League team folded several years ago.

The new Charros play in a new and modern stadium located in Zapopan, the venue was originally built as a track and field stadium for the 2011 Pan-American Games, but in 2014 it was adapted for baseball and the team became an instant success as Charros reached the final in their first season, but eventually lost to Culiacán in five games.

The venue hosted in 2017 the World Classic Series and in 2018 it will host the Serie del Caribe, these events are evidence that Guadalajara is a great city for baseball. To better accommodate the fans that will come from all over the country, the stadium will have an expansion that will take the capacity up to 16 thousand fans.

43. Visit the city's new aquarium

Guadalajara has a new attraction, Acuario Michín opened in March 2017 and has already met great reviews. The goal of the aquarium is to educate about the marvels of underwater life and vegetation.

Mexico has a long coastline and has great biodiversity along those shores, Acuario Michín displays all of it through its modern and ambitious project. It is considered the biggest aquarium in the country.

The aquarium is located in a very centric area just north of downtown Guadalajara, in the northwestern corner of the famous Parque Alcalde.

As of now the Line 1 of the electric train leaves you a couple of blocks away, but the upcoming Line 3 will also leave you within walking distance of Acuario Michín.

If you are into nature then you have to make a visit to one of our newest tourist attractions.

44. Guadalajara has a great zoo as well!

The city has an amazing zoo that I think is really underrated, people do visit and enjoy the place, but for some strange reason, it's never among the city's most valued places.

The zoo opened its doors in 1988 and is located in the far north zone of the city, at the edge, literally.

In 2005 the zoo started operating a safari type attraction that has been very well received by the public, you'll find giraffes, zebras, buffaloes, and white rhinos.

There is also a reptile exhibit that is considered the largest of its kind in Latin America, you'll find lizards, turtles, crocodiles, and snakes.

The bird exhibit is very cool too, it is formed by two steel pyramids that are inhabited by tropical birds in a controlled environment.

Of course, there is more, but I can't mention them all here, so go give our zoo a visit!

45. Local Markets Are The Soul of Guadalajara

I know that markets have been mentioned several times in this guide, but their importance in the city's social life is huge. They are not only buildings, they are the foundation of social unity, they have a financial and cultural impact in their communities, they promote interaction in the area they are located, and some of them are historically transcendent.

Local markets are integrated with the landscape, they normally have a plaza and a church next to them and serve as a town center, and that makes the visit worthwhile.

I already wrote about the most important one of all, Mercado Libertad (or San Juan de Dios), but there are many others that can be admired by their architectonic quality, such as Mercado San Antonio, Mercado Alcalde, Mercado San Diego, Mercado IV Centenario, Mercado Ayuntamiento, Mercado Juárez, Mercado Corona, Mercado General Eugenio Zuñiga, and Mercado de las Flores. All of them located in the Guadalajara municipality.

46. Visit Guadalajara's Urban Forest!

El Bosque (forest) de Los Colomos is one of the most beautiful sites in the city. It is Guadalajara's urban forest and where many families go for their picnics and to spend some quality time. It is also a popular spot for those who like to jog or simply walk.

Colomos has a lake with ducks, a Japanese Garden, and a cultural and recreational center where you can find drawing, painting, sculpture, and dancing lessons. You can also rent a horse and take a ride around the park.

This natural beauty is very easy to access, it is located on the border of the Zapopan and Guadalajara municipalities, in the northwestern part of town. It is connected by two of the most important avenues: Patria and Américas.

Take a breather from all the urban chaos and give yourself a chance to visit this spectacular site.

47. Go To The Most Famous Towns Outside Of The City: Tequila And Chapala

Tequila is one of the most popular tourist destinations in the country and it's only an hour drive from Guadalajara. It is famous for being the region where Tequila was created and where the most famous distilleries are located. Some of these distilleries are located in haciendas that have a very nostalgic feel and are historic buildings, where generations of families have lived.

Then we have Lake Chapala, the biggest lake of Mexico. There are several interesting towns around the lake and they are popular because they are beautiful sites to pass a nice quiet day or two.

Chapala is the most famous of them, you can find many great seafood restaurants and walk by the lake and take great pictures. Ajijic is also a great spot to visit, it is a beautiful and very colorful town that has great places to eat as well.

48. Go To A Concert In Teatro Degollado!

I will end this fifty tips guide on the more cultural side of Guadalajara, and Teatro Degollado is the symbol of cultural activities in the city. This theater is Guadalajara's most important cultural asset and it's the oldest of its kind operating in Mexico.

Teatro Degollado is home to the Philharmonic Orchestra of Jalisco and it has guided tours if you don't have the chance to attend a concert.

The building has a neoclassical façade and is one the most beautiful in all Guadalajara. It is located in downtown and it's one of the more recognizable constructions, it's just a block away from the cathedral.

It was opened in 1866 and it holds a capacity of 1015 people who can enjoy an opera, classical ballet, recitals, plays, mariachi galas, and concerts from world-class artists.

49. Go To The City's International Book Fair

One of Guadalajara's main international events is FIL (Feria Internacional del Libro, in Spanish). FIL is considered Latin America's biggest and most important book fair. People from all over the world come to Jalisco's capital to do business and they also get a taste of the best the city has to offer.

But locals also enjoy the book fair, because they can find rare editions and titles from countries all over the planet. Be it academic studies or the most recent bestseller, you will find it in FIL.

FIL is not only about books, it is a cultural event that has concerts with world-class artists and other academic activities. There is usually a guest country or region of the world that showcases the best of their culture, and that makes it very interesting. FIL usually starts in the last week of November and ends in the first week of December.

If you are a book lover that happens to be in town on those exact dates, don't think about it twice and visit FIL.

50. Go To The Guadalajara Film Festival

If you are a cinema lover and happen to be in town in March then you must go to the International Film Festival in Guadalajara. Known as the FICG, this is another important event in the city's cultural landscape. It is one of the most prominent spaces in which new films are promoted and exhibited to the world. A special emphasis is made in national and Latin American films.

The festival has a thirty-year existence (it started in 1986) and is already considered the most solid of its kind in Latin America. Filmmakers and professional related to the industry from all over the world gather and exchange experiences with films students and the new waves of actors and directors. The festival is very popular among cinema fans, who pack the theaters and appreciate the quality of the films.

The current name was adopted in 2001 when it officially evolved into a festival, a category it has maintained from that year to the present day.

Top Reasons to Book This Trip

- **Buildings and Monuments:** Historic masterpieces.

- **Food**: The best and most traditional dishes.

- **Mexican identity**: This the most Mexican city.

.

> TOURIST

GREATER THAN A TOURIST

Visit GreaterThanATourist.com
http://GreaterThanATourist.com

Sign up for the Greater Than a Tourist Newsletter
http://eepurl.com/cxspyf

Follow us on Facebook:
https://www.facebook.com/GreaterThanATourist

Follow us on Pinterest:
http://pinterest.com/GreaterThanATourist

Follow us on Instagram:
http://Instagram.com/GreaterThanATourist

> TOURIST

GREATER THAN A TOURIST

Please leave your honest review of this book on Amazon and Goodreads. Thank you.

We appreciate your positive and negative feedback as we try to provide tourist guidance in their next trip from a local.

Our Story

Traveling is a passion of the "Greater than a Tourist" series creator. Lisa studied abroad in college, and for their honeymoon Lisa and her husband toured Europe. During her travels to Malta, an older man tried to give her some advice based on his own experience living on the island since he was a young boy. She was not sure if she should talk to the stranger but was interested in his advice. When traveling to some places she was wary to talk to locals because she was afraid that they weren't being genuine. Through her travels, Lisa learned how much locals had to share with tourists. Lisa created the "Greater Than a Tourist" book series to help connect people with locals. A topic that locals are very passionate about sharing.

Notes

Made in the USA
Monee, IL
27 June 2023

37814399R10052